D1797600

THIS BOOK

To Isabella

with love

Freda & Jim Mclachlan

all Saints

Childwall

A Book
of Bible Verses

TO KEEP FOR EVER

Compiled by Sophie Piper
Illustrated by Ian Mitchell

A LION BOOK

Compiled by Sophie Piper
Illustrations copyright © 2002 Ian Mitchell
This edition copyright © 2002 Lion Hudson

The moral rights of the author and illustrator
have been asserted

A Lion Book
an imprint of
Lion Hudson plc
Mayfield House, 256 Banbury Road,
Oxford OX2 7DH, England
www.lionhudson.com
ISBN 0 7459 4756 5

First edition 2002
10 9 8 7 6 5 4 3

Acknowledgments
The Scripture quotations on pp. 11, 13, 19, 21, 22, 23, 25, 28, 32, 33, 34, 37, 38,
42, 45, 48, 53, 55, 58, 63, 64, 68, 70, 72, 78, 80, 81, 82, 84, 88, 89, 93, are from
The New Revised Standard Version of the Bible, Anglicized Edition, copyright ©
1989, 1995 by the Division of Christian Education of the National Council of the
Churches of Christ in the United States of America, and are used by permission.
All rights reserved. Scriptures quoted on pp. 10, 26, 29, 31, 32, 46, 47, 48, 49, 50,
51, 52, 52, 56, 57, 58, 60, 61, 76, 86, 90 from the Good News Bible published by
The Bible Societies/HarperCollins Publishers Ltd, UK © American Bible Society
1966, 1971, 1976, 1992, used with permission. Scripture quotations on pp. 9,
14, 16, 24, 54, 74, 91, 92 taken from the Holy Bible, New International Version,
copyright © 1973, 1978, 1984 by International Bible Society. Used by permission
of Hodder & Stoughton Limited. All rights reserved. 'NIV' is a registered trademark
of International Bible Society. UK trademark number 1448790. Extracts on pp. 18,
46, 59, 69, 73, 83 from the Revised English Bible, copyright © Oxford University
Press and Cambridge University Press 1989.

A catalogue record for this book is available
from the British Library

Typeset in 14/18 Venetian 301 BT
Printed and bound in China

Contents

Introduction

The Bible is the book of the Christian faith.

It is a collection of writings from long ago – a mixture of stories and tales and poems and wise sayings. It is the heritage of people who believe in God and who want to live in the way that pleases God. They read the Bible to find help and guidance and encouragement.

This selection of verses will introduce you to the wisdom of the Bible. May this be a faithful companion to you on your journey and lead you in the way of goodness.

What Does it Mean to be Wise?

How much better to get wisdom than gold,
to choose understanding rather than silver!

Proverbs 16:16

Where, then, is the source of wisdom?
Where can we learn to understand?

God alone knows the way,
Knows the place where wisdom is found,
Because he sees the ends of the earth,
Sees everything under the sky.
When God gave the wind its power
And determined the size of the sea;
When God decided where the rain would fall,
And the path that the thunderclouds travel;
It was then he saw wisdom and tested its
    worth —
He gave it his approval.

God said to human beings,
'To be wise, you must have reverence for
   the Lord.
To understand, you must turn from evil.'

Job 28:20, 23–28

You shall love the Lord your God with all
your heart, and with all your soul, and with
all your might.

Deuteronomy 6:5

THE BIBLE

SAYS

God is the Maker
of the World

The earth is the Lord's and all that is in it,
    the world, and those who live in it;
for he has founded it on the seas,
    and established it on the rivers.

Psalm 24:1–2

Praise the Lord.
Praise the Lord from the heavens;
   praise him in the heights above.
Praise him, all his angels,
   praise him, all his heavenly hosts.

Praise him, sun and moon,
   praise him, all you shining stars.
Praise him, you highest heavens,
   and you waters above the skies.
Let them praise the name of the Lord,
   for he commanded and they were created.
He set them in place for ever and ever;
   he gave a decree that will never pass away.

Praise the Lord from the earth,
   you great sea creatures and all ocean depths,

lightning and hail, snow and clouds,
   stormy winds that do his bidding,
you mountains and all hills,
   fruit trees and all cedars,
wild animals and all cattle,
small creatures and flying birds,
kings of the earth and all nations,
   you princes and all rulers on earth,
young men and maidens,
   old men and children!

Let them praise the name of the Lord,
   for his name alone is exalted;
   his splendour is above the earth and
      the heavens...
Praise the Lord.

Psalm 148 (abbreviated)

Give thanks to the Lord, for he is good.
His love endures for ever.
Give thanks to the God of gods.
His love endures for ever.
Give thanks to the Lord of lords:
His love endures for ever.
to him who alone does great wonders,
His love endures for ever.
who by his understanding made the
heavens,
His love endures for ever.
who spread out the earth upon the waters,
His love endures for ever.
who made the great lights –
His love endures for ever.

the sun to govern the day,
His love endures for ever.
the moon and stars to govern the night...
His love endures for ever.

Give thanks to the God of heaven.
His love endures for ever.

Psalm 136:1–9, 26

You care for the earth and make it fruitful;
you enrich it greatly,
filling its great channels with rain.
In this way you prepare the earth
and provide grain for its people.
You water its furrows, level its ridges,
soften it with showers, and bless its growth.
You crown the year with your good gifts;
places where you have passed drip with plenty;
the open pastures are lush
and the hills wreathed in happiness;
the meadows are clothed with sheep
and the valleys decked with grain,
so that with shouts of joy they break into
    song.

Psalm 65:9–13

The earth had yielded its increase;
   God, our God, has blessed us.
May God continue to bless us;
   let all the ends of the earth revere him.

Psalm 67:6–7

THE BIBLE

SAYS

God is Love

God is love, and those who abide
in love abide in God, and God
abides in them.

1 John 4:16

Your steadfast love, O Lord, extends to
   the heavens,
your faithfulness to the clouds.
Your righteousness is like the mighty
   mountains,
your judgements are like the great deep;
you save humans and animals alike, O Lord.

How precious is your steadfast love, O God!

Psalm 36:5–7

Satisfy us in the morning with your
    steadfast love,
so that we may rejoice and be glad all
    our days.

Psalm 90:14

I will be a Father to you,
    and you will be my sons and daughters,
    says the Lord Almighty.

2 Corinthians 6:18

Jesus said:

'Let the little children come to me, and do not stop them; for it is to such as these that the kingdom of God belongs. Truly I tell you, whoever does not receive the kingdom of God as a little child will never enter it.'

Luke 18:16–17

Jesus called a child and said to his disciples:
'See that you don't despise any of these
little ones. Their angels in heaven, I tell
you, are always in the presence of my Father
in heaven.

   'What do you think a man does who has a
hundred sheep and one of them gets lost?
He will leave the other ninety-nine grazing
on the hillside and go and look for the lost
sheep. When he finds it, I tell you, he feels
far happier over this one sheep than over
the ninety-nine that did not get lost. In just
the same way your Father in heaven does
not want any of these little ones to be lost.'

Matthew 18:10–14

Jesus said:

'Blessed are the poor in spirit, for theirs is the kingdom of heaven.

'Blessed are those who mourn, for they will be comforted.

'Blessed are the meek, for they will inherit the earth.

'Blessed are those who hunger and thirst for righteousness, for they will be filled.

'Blessed are the merciful, for they will receive mercy.

'Blessed are the pure in heart, for they will see God.

'Blessed are the peacemakers, for they will be called children of God.

'Blessed are those who are persecuted for righteousness' sake, for theirs is the kingdom of heaven.

'Blessed are you when people revile you and persecute you and utter all kinds of evil against you falsely on my account. Rejoice and be glad, for your reward is great in heaven.'

Matthew 5:3–12

Show me how much you love me, Lord, and save me according to your promise.

Psalm 119:41

God Hears Our Prayers

Don't worry about anything, but in all your prayers ask God for what you need, always asking him with a thankful heart.

Philippians 4:6

I pray to you, O Lord;
  you hear my voice in the morning;
at sunrise I offer my prayer
  and wait for your answer.

Psalm 5:2–3

Jesus said:

'Whenever you pray, go into your room and shut the door and pray to your Father who is in secret; and your Father who sees in secret will reward you.'

Matthew 6:6

Jesus said:

'Ask, and it will be given to you; search, and you will find; knock, and the door will be opened for you. For everyone who asks receives, and everyone who searches finds, and for everyone who knocks, the door will be opened.'

Matthew 7:7–8

33

Jesus said:
'Your Father knows what you need before
you ask him.

　'Pray then in this way:

　'Our Father in heaven,
　　hallowed be your name.
　　Your kingdom come.
　　Your will be done,
　　on earth as it is in heaven.
　　Give us this day our daily bread.
　　And forgive us our debts,
　　as we also have forgiven our debtors.
　　And do not bring us to the time of trial,
　　but rescue us from the evil one.

'For if you forgive others their trespasses, your heavenly Father will also forgive you; but if you do not forgive others, neither will your Father forgive your trespasses.'

Matthew 6:8–15

God spoke all these words:

I am the Lord your God... you shall have no
  other gods before me.

You shall not make for yourself any idols...

You shall not bow down to them or worship
  them...

You shall not make wrongful use of the name
  of the Lord your God...

Remember the sabbath day, and keep it
  holy...

Honour your father and your mother...

You shall not murder.

You shall not commit adultery.

You shall not steal.
You shall not bear false witness against
  your neighbour.
You shall not covet… anything that
  belongs to your neighbour.

Exodus 20:1–17 (adapted)

Jesus said:

'For God so loved the world that he gave his only Son, so that everone who believes in him may not perish but may have eternal life.

'Indeed, God did not send the Son into the world to condemn the world, but in order that the world might be saved through him. Those who believe in him are not condemned; but those who do not believe are condemned already, because they have not believed in the name of the only Son of God. And this is the judgement, that the light has come into the world, and people loved darkness rather than light because their deeds were evil. For all who do evil hate the light and do not come to the light, so that their deeds may not be exposed. But those who do what is true come to the light, so that it may be clearly seen that their deeds have been done in God.'

John 3:16–21

THE BIBLE

PRAISES

Wise Living

The fruit of the Spirit is love, joy, peace, patience, kindness, generosity, faithfulness, gentleness, and self-control.

Galatians 5:22–23

It is your own face that you see reflected in the water and it is your own self that you see in your heart.

Proverbs 27:19

Anyone who listens to the message but does not act on it is like somebody looking in a mirror at the face nature gave him; he glances at himself and goes his way, and promptly forgets what he looked like. But he who looks into the perfect law, the law that makes us free, and does not turn away, remembers what he hears; he acts on it, and by so acting he will find happiness.

James 1:23–25

Do not conform yourselves to the standards of this world, but let God transform you inwardly by a complete change of your mind. Then you will be able to know the will of God – what is good and is pleasing to him and is perfect.

Romans 12:2

Do not imitate what is evil, but imitate what is good.

3 John:11

Jesus said:
'No good tree bears bad fruit, nor again does a bad tree bear good fruit; for each tree is known by its own fruit. Figs are not gathered from thorns, nor are grapes picked from a bramble bush. The good person out of the good treasure of the heart produces good, and the evil person out of evil treasure produces evil.'

Luke 6:43–45

You will earn the trust and respect of others if you work for good; if you work for evil, you are making a mistake.

Proverbs 14:22

Those who are good travel a road that avoids evil; so watch where you are going – it may save your life.

Proverbs 16:17

Be kind and honest and you will live a long life; others will respect you and treat you fairly.

Proverbs 21:21

If you are lazy, you will meet difficulty everywhere, but if you are honest, you will have no trouble.

Proverbs 15:19

Work and you will earn a living; if you sit round talking you will be poor.

Proverbs 14:23

Your reward depends on what you say and what you do; you will get what you deserve.

Proverbs 12:14

It is better to have a little, honestly earned, than to have a large income gained dishonestly.

Proverbs 16:8

Be wise enough not to wear yourself out trying to get rich. Your money can be gone in a flash, as if it had grown wings and flown away like an eagle.

Proverbs 23:4

Of course, there is great gain in godliness combined with contentment; for we brought nothing into the world – it is certain that we can take nothing out of it; but if we have food and clothing, we will be content with these.

But those who want to be rich fall into temptation and are trapped by many senseless and harmful desires that plunge people into ruin and destruction. For the love of money is a root of all kinds of evil, and in their eagerness to be rich some have wandered away from the faith and pierced themselves with many pains.

1 Timothy 6:6–10

Jesus said:

'Therefore I tell you, do not worry about your life, what you will eat; or about your body, what you will wear. Life is more than food, and the body more than clothes. Consider the ravens: they do not sow nor reap, they have no storeroom or barn; yet God feeds them. And how much more valuable you are than birds! Who of you by worrying can add a single hour to his life? Since you cannot do this very little thing, why do you worry about the rest?

  'Consider how the lilies grow. They do not labour or spin. Yet I tell you, not even Solomon in all his splendour was dressed like one of these. If that is how God clothes the grass of the field, which is here today, and tomorrow is thrown into the fire, how much more will he clothe you, O you of little faith!'

Luke 12:22–28

Jesus said:
'Do not store up for yourselves treasure on earth, where moth and rust consume and where thieves break in and steal; but store up for yourselves treasures in heaven where neither moth nor rust consumes and where thieves do not break in and steal. For where your treasure is, there your heart will be also.'

Matthew 6:19–21

Do not use harmful words, but only helpful words, the kind that build up and provide what is needed, so that what you say will do good to those who hear you.

Ephesians 4:29

A person's words can be a source of wisdom, deep as the ocean, fresh as a flowing stream.

Proverbs 18:4

A gentle answer quietens anger, but a harsh one stirs it up.

Proverbs 15:1

A lie has a short life, but truth lives for ever.

Proverbs 12:19

Do not fret because of the wicked;
  do not be envious of wrongdoers,
for they will soon fade like the grass…

Trust in the Lord, and do good.

Psalm 37:1–3 (abbreviated)

People with a hot temper do foolish things;
wiser people remain calm.

Proverbs 14:17

Don't take it on yourself to repay a wrong.
Trust the Lord and he will make it right.

Proverbs 20:22

Put on, then, garments that suit God's
chosen and beloved people: compassion,
kindness, humility, gentleness, patience.
Be tolerant with one another and forgiving,
if any of you has cause for complaint: you
must forgive as the Lord forgave you.
Finally, to bind everything together and
complete the whole, there must be love.

Colossians 3:12–14

Listen to your father; without him you would not exist. When your mother is old, show her your appreciation.

Proverbs 23:22

Homes are built on the foundation of wisdom and understanding. Where there is knowledge, the rooms are furnished with valuable, beautiful things.

Proverbs 24:3–4

If you want people to like you, forgive them when they wrong you. Remembering wrongs can break up a friendship.

Proverbs 17:9

An honest answer is a sign of true friendship.

Proverbs 24:26

Love Your Neighbour

Jesus said:
'In everything do to others as you would
have them do to you; for this is the law and
the prophets.'

Matthew 7:12

A lawyer stood up to test Jesus. 'Teacher,' he said, 'what must I do to inherit eternal life?' He said to him, 'What is written in the law? What do you read there?' He answered, 'You shall love the Lord your God with all your heart and with all your soul, and with all your strength, and with all your mind; and your neighbour as yourself.' And he said to him, 'You have given the right answer; do this, and you will live.'

But wanting to justify himself, he asked Jesus, 'And who is my neighbour?'

Jesus replied, 'A man was going down from Jerusalem to Jericho, and fell into the hands of robbers, who stripped him, beat him, and

went away, leaving him half dead. Now by chance a priest was going down that road; and when he saw him, he passed by on the other side. So likewise a Levite, when he came to the place and saw him, passed by on the other side. But a Samaritan while travelling came near him; and when he saw him, he was moved with pity. He went to him and bandaged his wounds, having poured oil and wine on them. Then he put him on his own animal, brought him to an inn, and took care of him. The next day he took out two denarii, gave them to the innkeeper, and said, "Take care of him; and when I come back, I will repay you whatever more you spend." Which of these three, do you think, was a neighbour to the man who fell into the hands of the robbers?' He said, 'The one who showed him mercy.' Jesus said to him, 'Go and do likewise.'

Luke 10:25–37

Happy are those who consider the poor;
the Lord delivers them in the day of trouble.

Psalm 41:1

Jesus said:

'When you are having guests for lunch or supper, do not invite your friends, your brothers or other relations, or your rich neighbours; they will only ask you back again and so you will be repaid. But when you give a party, ask the poor, the crippled, the lame, and the blind. That is the way to find happiness, because they have no means of repaying you. You will be repaid on the day when the righteous rise from the dead.'

Luke 14:12–14

Jesus said:

'I say to you that listen, love your enemies, do good to those who hate you, bless those who curse you, pray for those who abuse you. If anyone strikes you on the cheek, offer the other also; and from anyone who takes away your coat do not withhold even your shirt. Give to everyone who begs from you; and if anyone takes away your goods, do not ask for them again. Do to others as you would have them do to you...

'Do not judge, and you will not be judged; do not condemn, and you will not be condemned. Forgive, and you will be forgiven.

Luke 6:27–31, 37

Jesus said:

'I give you a new commandment, that you love one another. Just as I have loved you, you also should love one another. By this everyone will know that you are my disciples, if you have love for one another.'

John 13:34–35

My dear friends, let us love one another, because the source of love is God. Everyone who loves is a child of God and knows God, but the unloving know nothing of God, for God is love. This is how he showed his love among us: he sent his only Son into the world that we might have life through him. This is what love really is: not that we have loved God, but that he loved us and sent his Son as a sacrifice to atone for our sins.

1 John 4:7–10

Love is patient, love is kind. It does not envy, it does not boast, it is not proud. It is not rude, it is not self-seeking, it is not easily angered, it keeps no record of wrongs. Love does not delight in evil but rejoices with the truth. It always protects, always trusts, always hopes, always perseveres.

Love never fails. But where there are prophecies, they will cease; where there are tongues, they will be stilled; where there is knowledge, it will pass away. For we know in part and we prophesy in part, but when perfection comes, the imperfect disappears. When I was a child, I talked like a child, I thought like a child, I reasoned like a child.

When I became a man, I put childish ways behind me. Now we see but a poor reflection as in a mirror; then we shall see face to face. Now I know in part; then I shall know fully, even as I am fully known.

And now these three remain: faith, hope and love. But the greatest of these is love.

1 Corinthians 13:4–13

Trust in God

God loves you, so don't let anything worry
you or frighten you.

Daniel 10:19

Why are you cast down, O my soul,
and why are you disquieted within me?
Hope in God; for I shall again praise him,
my help and my God.

Psalm 42:5

The Lord is near to the broken-hearted,
and saves the crushed in spirit.

Psalm 34:18

Have you not known? Have you not heard?
The Lord is the everlasting God,
 the Creator of the ends of the earth.
He does not faint or grow weary;
 his understanding is unsearchable.
He gives power to the faint,
 and strengthens the powerless.
Even youths will faint and be weary,
 and the young will fall exhausted;
but those who wait for the Lord shall renew
 their strength,
 they shall mount up with wings like eagles,
they shall run and not be weary,
 they shall walk and not faint.

Isaiah 40:28–31

The Lord is my light and my salvation;
  whom shall I fear?
The Lord is the stronghold of my life;
  of whom shall I be afraid?

Psalm 27:1

The Lord is my rock, my fortress, and my
  deliverer,
  my God, my rock in whom I take refuge.

Psalm 18:2

God is our refuge and our stronghold,
a timely help in trouble;
so we are not afraid though the earth shakes
and the mountains move in the depths of
    the sea,
when its waters seethe in tumult
and the mountains quake before its majesty.

Psalm 46:1–3

The Lord is my shepherd, I shall not want.
    He makes me lie down in green pastures;
he leads me beside still waters;
    he restores my soul.
He leads me in right paths
    for his name's sake.

Even though I walk through the darkest valley,
    I fear no evil;
for you are with me;
    your rod and your staff –
    they comfort me.

You prepare a table before me
    in the presence of my enemies;
you anoint my head with oil;
    my cup overflows.

Surely goodness and mercy shall follow me
   all the days of my life,
and I shall dwell in the house of the Lord
   my whole life long.

Psalm 23

THE BIBLE

SAYS

God's Love is For Ever

We wait for what God has promised:
new heavens and a new earth, where
righteousness will be at home.

2 Peter 3:13

I am convinced that neither death, nor life, nor angels, nor rulers, nor things present, nor things to come, nor powers, nor height, nor depth, nor anything else in all creation, will be able to separate us from the love of God in Christ Jesus our Lord.

Romans 8:38–39

Jesus said:

'Do not let your hearts be troubled. Believe in God, believe also in me. In my Father's house there are many dwelling-places. If it were not so, would I have told you that I go to prepare a place for you? And if I go and prepare a place for you, I will come again and will take you to myself, so that where I am, there you may be also.'

John 14:1–3

This is how it will be when the dead are raised to life. When the body is buried, it is mortal; when raised, it will be immortal. When buried, it is ugly and weak; when raised, it will be beautiful and strong.

So when this takes place, and the mortal has been changed into the immortal, then the scripture will come true: 'Death is destroyed; victory is complete!'

1 Corinthians 15:42–43, 54

Then I saw a new heaven and a new earth, for the first heaven and the first earth had passed away, and there was no longer any sea. I saw the Holy City, the new Jerusalem, coming down out of heaven from God, prepared as a bride beautifully dressed for her husband. And I heard a loud voice from the throne saying, 'Now the dwelling of God is with men, and he will live with them. They will be his people, and God himself will be with them and be their God. He will wipe every tear from their eyes. There will be no more death or mourning or crying or pain, for the old order of things has passed away.

Revelation 21:1–4

Finally… whatever is true, whatever is noble, whatever is right, whatever is pure, whatever is lovely, whatever is admirable – if anything is excellent or praiseworthy – think about such things. Whatever you have learned or received or heard from me, or seen in me – put it into practice. And the God of peace will be with you.

Philippians 4:8–9

Jesus said:
'Peace I leave with you; my peace I give to you.'

John 14:27

By day the Lord commands his steadfast love,
and at night his song is with me,
a prayer to the God of my life.

Psalm 42:8

Index of Bible References